PRAISE MY PET:

ADULT COLORING BOOK

WWW.PRAISEMYPET.COM

Color Shasta and Gizzy!

Color Ginger!

Color Ewok, Lilly, Daisy and Winston!

7

Color Jetta, Gwen and Marley!

Color Guppy!

Color Rudy and Louise!

Color Milo, Maddy and Marvin!

Color Trouble Marie and Pepper!

Color Toby!

13

Color Blu and Bella!

17

Color Loki!

Color Princess and Bailey!

18

Color Little Bit and Mossy!

Color Annie, Foxy Girl,
Ruby Reds and Kyle!

23

Color Chip, Kayoyoko and Princess!

28

Color Roxi, Chaos and Tig!

29

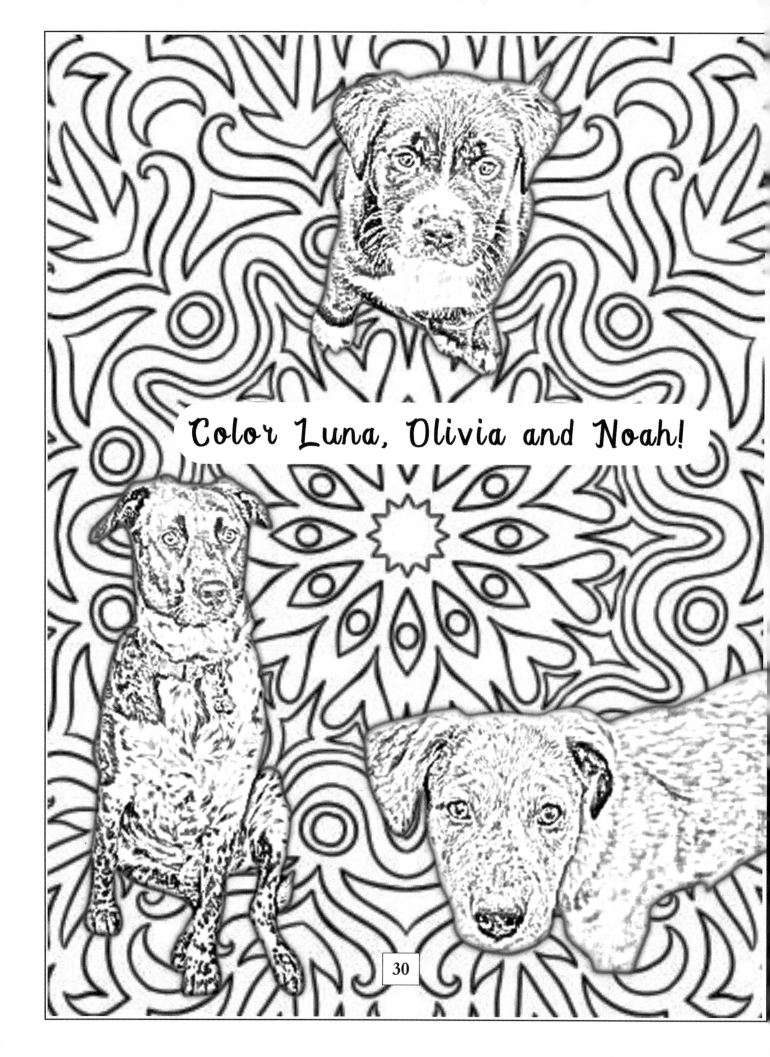

Color Luna, Olivia and Noah!

Color Daisy, Tiva and Diesel!

33

Color Jack, Sadie and Hedie!

34

Color Otis!

Color Heidi and Jasper!

Color Coco and Karma!

Color Rosie and Lizzie!

39

Color Kisser, Venom, Shadowmoon, Tigress and Katie!

Color Gigi, Daisy and Lilly!

Color Sabrina and Chase!

Color Kipper!

42

Color Ace!

Color Peeka and Mccoy!

43

Color Twilight and Titan!

Color Bubba!

Color Calvin and Jamaica!

Color Maggie Mae and Lola Pearl!

45

Color Kirk!

Color Coal!

46

Color Precious, Cute Pie and Buddy!

Color Lucky Luciano and Bugsy Siegel!

Color Fritz!

49

Color Lucy, Pippa, Watson, Lady A and Toby!

54

Color Ollie!

Color Mina!

Color Dakota!

55

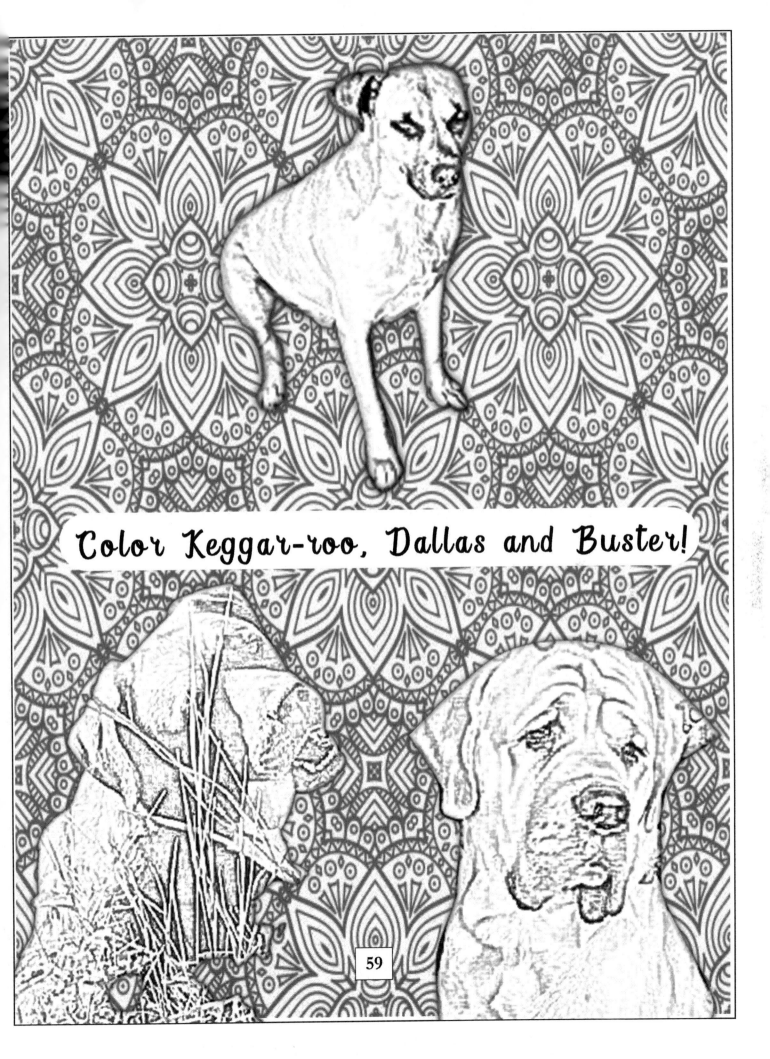

Color Keggar-roo, Dallas and Buster!

59

Color Spike, Oreo, Sadie, Gizmo and Nanook!

Color Diva and Tinker!

Color Scooby Sue!

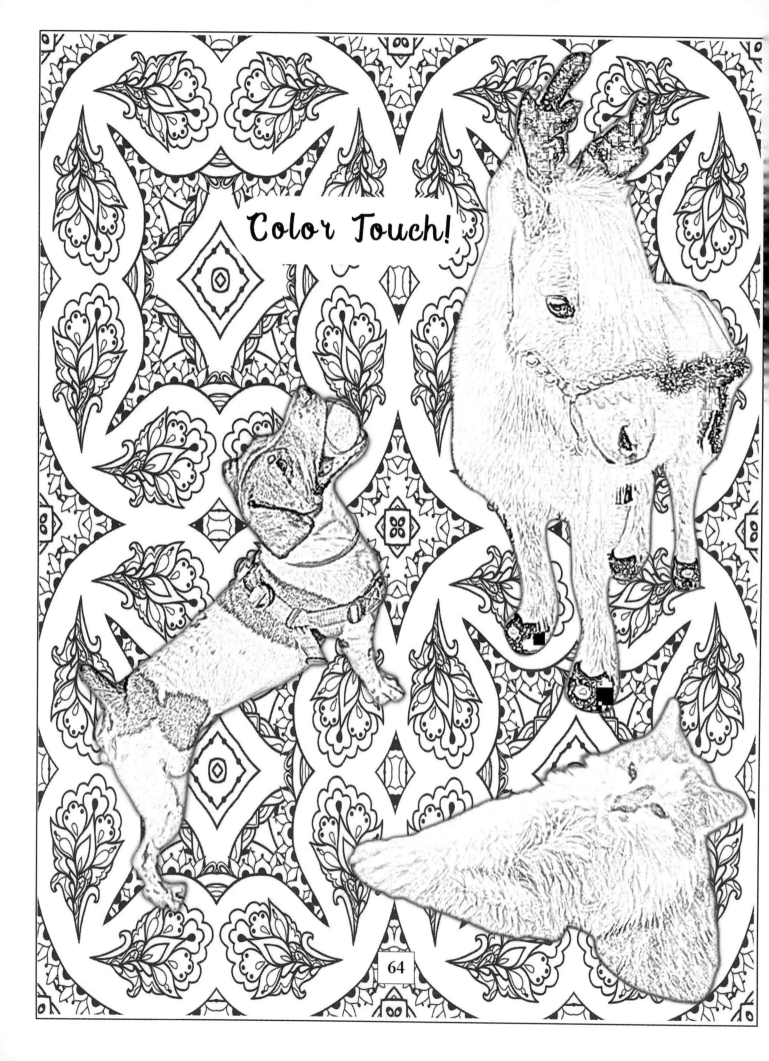

Color Touch!

Color Crash!

Color Missy Sue!

Color Queenie!

67

Color Bozy!

Color Sirena Sky and Athena!

68

Color Chewie, Tiger, Caliber and Blanca!

70

Color Cody and Rocky!

Color Bailey!

Color Brodie Crackers!

Color Mollymae!

Color Carmel!

Color Smokie, Sophie and Lokie!

Color Tilly, Meesha and Mei-Ling!

77

Color Nova, Goose, Java and Moose!

Color Lord Duc and Lady Grace!

80

Color Wiggles and Koda!

Color Harley!

Color Karma!

83

Color Pockets, Hank, Minx and Myla!

Color Oakley Rae!

Color Winston!

85

Color Bella and Charlie!

Color Scooby and Scrappy!

89

Color Sadza and Sharik!

Color Belle and Billy!

Color Zsazzy!

93

Color Mugzee!

Color Rocky and Captain!

95

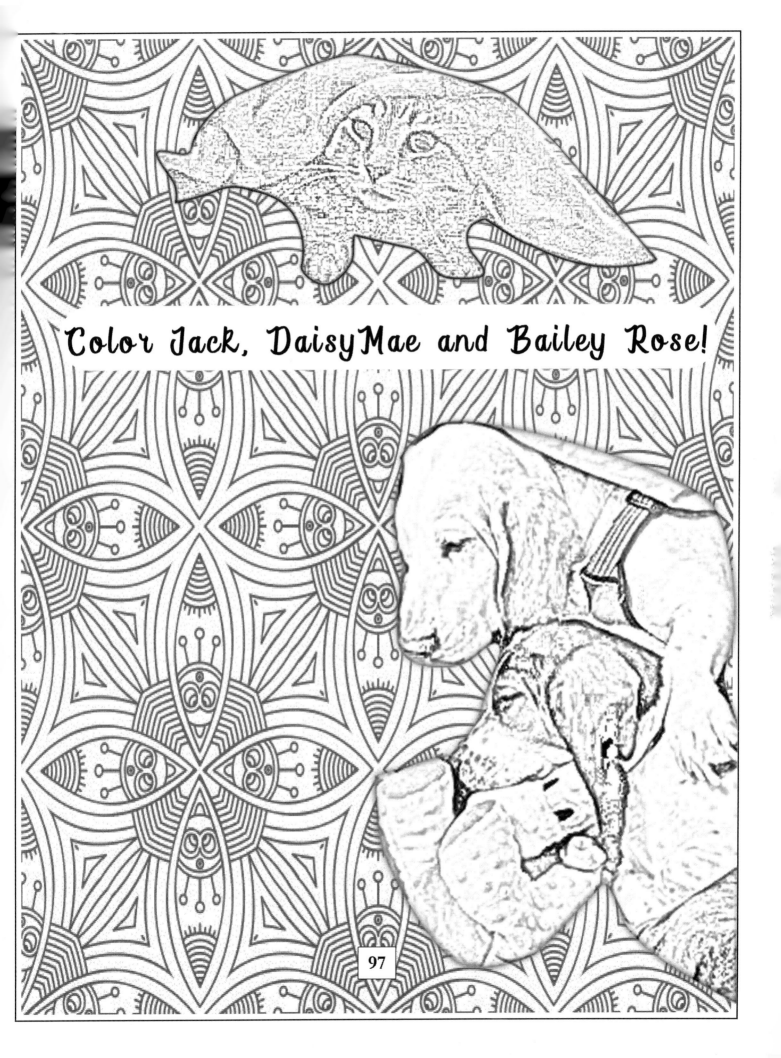

Color Jack, DaisyMae and Bailey Rose!

Color Grazie and Massimo!

98

Color Murphy!

Color Bentley Lee and Kimba!

100

Color Jack, Tipper and Mrytle!

Color Lil Dude!

We hope you enjoyed our coloring book! If you'd like to see YOUR pet in one of our upcoming coloring books, visit www.praisemypet.com/pages/send-us-your-pet-photos

Happy coloring!

Made in the USA
Columbia, SC
19 February 2021